Celebrations

Celebraciones

Les Fêtes

慶祝

text by Jocelyn Graeme
photos by Ruth Fahlman, May Henderson, and Kristin Colwell

Addison-Wesley Publishers Limited
Don Mills, Ontario • Reading, Massachusetts
Menlo Park, California • New York
Wokingham, England • Amsterdam • Bonn
Sydney • Singapore • Tokyo • Madrid • San Juan

Holidays are special! There are so many things to do.

C'est chouette, les fêtes! Voilà ce que nous pouvons faire.

Las festividades son días especiales! Hay tantas cosas que hacer.

假期是特別的，並且可以做很多的事。

We listen to the call of a shofar on Rosh Hashanah.

Nous écoutons l'appel d'un shofar à Rosh Hashanah.

Escuchamos el sonido del cuerno en Rosh Hashanah.

我們聽到 "手花" 在 Rosh Hashanah。

We smell a Thanksgiving turkey fresh from the oven.

Nous sentons l'odeur d'une dinde qui sort du four à l'Action de grâce.

Olemos el aroma de un pavo al horno en el Día de Gracia.

我們聞到剛出烤爐的感恩節火雞。

We surprise the jack-o-lanterns that smile on Halloween.

Nous surprenons les citrouilles qui sourient à l'halloween.

Sorprendemos las calabazas iluminadas que sonríen en el Día de las brujas.

我們驚訝鬼皇節的微笑燈籠。

We taste the sweetness of Diwali treats.

Nous nous offrons le goût sucré des friandises à la Diwali.

Saboreamos el gusto de los dulces Diwalis.

我們吃到 Diwali 的甜品。

We listen to a choir singing Christmas songs.

Nous écoutons un choeur qui chante des chansons de Noël.

Escuchamos a un coro que canta canciones navideñas.

我們聽到詩班唱的聖誕歌。

We watch the fierce lion dancing on Chinese New Year.

Nous regardons danser le lion féroce au jour de l'An chinois.

Miramos al león feroz que danza en el Año Nuevo Chino.

我們看到中國新年的舞獅。

We taste the paskha that's baked for Easter.

Nous goûtons au paskha qu'on fait cuire à Pâques.

Saboreamos la paskha que se cocina para Semana Santa.

我們吃到復活節的"百是加"。

We smell the fragrance of May Day flowers.

Nous sentons le parfum des fleurs du premier mai.

Olemos el aroma de las flores del Primero de Mayo.

我們聞到五月的花香。

We nibble our way through Potlatch bannock.

Nous grignotons du bannock au Potlatch.

Mordisqueamos Potlatch bannock.

我們一路細嚼 "保那" 米餅。

And on Canada Day, we celebrate the holiday together.

Et le jour de la fête du Canada, nous fêtons tous ensemble.

Y en el Día de Canadá celebramos juntos la festividad.

在加拿大國慶日，我們一起慶祝假期。

Sponsoring Editor: Beth Bruder

Designer: Pamela Kinney

Editor: Lauren E. Wolk

Translators
Spanish: Edith Stagni
          Brenda Cortes

French: Katherine Stauble
        Martine Brassard

Chinese: Mei-lin Cheung
         Sew Pim Lim
         Hsiao Chiang

Sponsor: Early Childhood Multicultural Services
Early Childhood Multicultural Services gratefully acknowledges the support and financial
assistance of the Multiculturalism Directorate, Secretary of State, Canada; the Cabinet
Committee on Cultural Heritage, Province of British Columbia; and the Preschool ESL
Committee (PRESL), Vancouver.

Canadian Cataloguing in Publication Data

Graeme, Jocelyn, 1958–
  Celebrations

(Hand in hand)
Text in English, Chinese, French, Spanish.
ISBN 0-201-54650-7 (set). – ISBN 0-201-54656-6 (School Edition)
ISBN 0-201-55415-1 (Trade Edition)

1. Holidays – Juvenile literature. 2. Fasts
and feasts – Juvenile literature.   I. Fahlman,
Ruth, 1954–   .   II. Henderson, May.   III. Colwell,
Kristin.   IV. Title.   V. Series: Hand in hand
(Don Mills, Ont.).

GT3933.G73 1990   394.2′6   C90-094225-8

ISBN 0-201-54656-6 (School Edition)   **ISBN 0-201-55415-1** (Trade Edition)

Printed in Canada

A B C D E F – ALG – 95 94 93 92 91 90